EVERY BRILLIANT THING

by DUNCAN MACMILLAN

with Jonny Donahoe

**The first performance of *Every Brilliant Thing*
took place on 28 June 2013 at Ludlow Fringe Festival.**

**PENTABUS
RURAL THEATRE COMPANY**

 Paines
Plough

 Supported by
**ARTS COUNCIL
ENGLAND**

by Duncan Macmillan
with Jonny Donahoe

Cast	Jonny Donahoe
Direction	George Perrin
Producer	Hanna Streeter
Line Producer	Francesca Moody
Stage Manager	Alicia White

Every Brilliant Thing was commissioned with the support of Anne McMeehan and Jim Roberts. It was produced and toured with the support of Arts Council England's Strategic Touring Fund.

TOUR DATES

2013

28 June Ludlow Fringe Festival

5 July Ledbury Poetry Festival

2014

19 May Pentabus, Shropshire

20 May The Hive, Worcester

21 May The Edge, Much Wenlock

23 May Whaddon Jubilee Hall, Buckinghamshire

5-22 August Roundabout @ Summerhall, Edinburgh Festival Fringe

4 September Roundabout @ Margate Winter Gardens

7 September Bestival, Isle of Wight

22-25 September Roundabout @ Hackney Downs Studios

6-31 December Barrow Street Theatre, New York

2015

1 January-29 March Barrow Street Theatre, New York

2-3 May Machynlleth Comedy Festival

9 May Unity Theatre, Liverpool

12-16 May Theatre Royal Plymouth

18 May The North Wall, Oxford

19-24 May Roundabout @ Brighton Festival

21 May Quarterhouse, Folkestone

22 May The Spring, Havant

26 May The Dukes, Lancaster

28 May Trestle Arts Base, St Albans

30 May Leintwardine Village Hall

2 June Pulse Festival, Ipswich

3 June The Brewery, Kendal

4 June Harlow Playhouse, Harlow

5-6 June The Marlowe Theatre, Canterbury

25 June The Phoenix, Bordon

7 June Square Chapel, Halifax

10 June Marine Theatre, Lyme Regis

11 June The Muni, Colne

12-13 June The Lowry, Salford

15 June South Hill Park, Bracknell

17 June The Castle, Wellingborough

18 June The Garage, Norwich

19 June Key Theatre, Peterborough

21 June The Tolmen Centre, Constantine

23 June Salisbury Arts Centre, Salisbury

26-27 June Derby Theatre, Derby

6 -11 July Roundabout @ Southbank Centre, London

10-30 August Roundabout @ Summerhall, Edinburgh Festival Fringe

9 Sept The Civic, Stourport on Severn

11 Sept Bridport Arts Centre, Dorset

16 Sept Mill Arts Centre, Banbury

21 Sept Isle of Eigg

23 Sept Arainn Shuainert, Strontian

24 Sept Plockton Village Hall

25 Sept Carigmonie Centre, Drumnadrochit

26 Sept Lyth Arts Centre

27 Sept Pier Arts Centre, Orkney

29 Sept Carraigeworks, Leeds

1 Oct South Holland Centre, Spalding

2-3 Oct Pegasus Theatre, Oxford

4 Oct Chipping Norton Theatre,

6-10 Oct Tobacco Factory, Bristol

16-17 Oct Stephen Joseph Theatre, Scarborough

14 Oct Stahl Theatre, Peterborough

18-20 Oct The Old Market, Brighton

21 Oct Shopfront Theatre, Coventry

22 Oct Span Arts, Narberth

23 Oct Riverfront Theatre, Newport

24 Oct Pontardawe Arts Centre

29 Oct Lakeside Theatre

31 Oct The Edge Theatre, Chorlton

BIOGRAPHIES

DUNCAN MACMILLAN
(Writer)

Duncan is a former Writer-in-Residence at Paines Plough and Manchester Royal Exchange. Plays include the acclaimed adaptation of George Orwell's 1984, co-adapted/co-directed with Robert Icke (Headlong / Nottingham Playhouse, UK tour, Almeida Theatre and West End); EVERY BRILLIANT THING (Paines Plough / Pentabus); 2071 co-written with Chris Rapley (Royal Court / Hamburg Schauspielhaus); REISE DURCH DIE NACHT adapt. Friederike Mayröcker created with Katie Mitchell and Lyndsey Turner (Schauspielhaus Köln, Theatertreffen, Festival d'Avignon); WUNSCHLOSES UNGLÜCK adapt. Peter Handke (Burgtheater Vienna); THE FORBIDDEN ZONE (Salzburg Festival / Schaubühne Berlin); LUNGS (Studio Theatre Washington DC / Paines Plough & Sheffield Theatres); ATMEN (Schaubühne Berlin); DON JUAN COMES BACK FROM THE WAR adapt. Ödön von Horváth (Finborough Theatre); MONSTER (Royal Exchange / Manchester International Festival).

Duncan was the recipient of two awards in the inaugural Bruntwood Playwriting Competition, 2006. Other awards include Best New Play at the Off West End Awards 2013 for LUNGS; the Big Ambition Award, Old Vic 2009; the Pearson Prize, 2008. His work with director Katie Mitchell has been selected for Theatertreffen and the Avignon Festival.

JONNY DONAHOE

Jonny Donahoe is an actor, comedian and writer, best known as the front man of comedy-band Jonny & the Baptists. As a comedian he has toured across the UK, Ireland and Europe.

Credits include: THE NOW SHOW, SKETCHORAMA, THE COMEDY CLUB and INFINITE MONKEY CAGE (Radio 4). TV credits include: FRESH FROM THE FRINGE (BBC TV), THE GADGET SHOW (Channel 5). Theatre credits include: MARCUS BRIGSTOCKE'S EARLY EDITION (Latitude Festival & Edinburgh Festival 2012) and 9 LESSONS & CAROLS FOR GODLESS PEOPLE (Bloomsbury Theatre).

He was a finalist in New Act of the Year, Musical Comedy Awards and BBC New Talent.

For Jonny and the Baptists he was commissioned to write and perform at the National Theatre, (and on a UK tour), as part of Mark Thomas's 100 ACTS OF MINOR DISSENT. One of the songs written for this was subsequently recorded and released as a UK single, sold out its entire run, and became number one in the iTunes UK comedy charts.

For his role in EVERY BRILLIANT THING he has been nominated for a Lucille Lortel Award and a Drama Desk Award.

GEORGE PERRIN (Direction)

George Perrin is the joint Artistic Director of Paines Plough. He was formerly co-founder and Joint Artistic Director of nabokov and Trainee Associate Director at Paines Plough and Watford Palace Theatre.

Directing credits for Paines Plough include LUNGS by Duncan Macmillan, THE INITIATE by Alexandra Wood, OUR TEACHER'S A TROLL by Dennis Kelly (Roundabout Season, Edinburgh Festival Fringe and National Tour), NOT THE WORST PLACE by Sam Burns (Sherman Cymru, Theatr Clwyd), SEA WALL by Simon Stephens (Dublin Theatre Festival / National Theatre Shed), GOOD WITH PEOPLE by David Harrower (59East59 Theatres New York / Traverse Theatre / Oran Mor), LONDON by Simon Stephens (National Tour), SIXTY-FIVE MILES by Matt Hartley (Hull Truck), THE 8TH by Ché Walker and Paul Heaton (Latitude Festival/ Barbican / Manchester International Festival / National Tour), DIG by Katie Douglas (Oran Mor / National Tour) and JUICY FRUITS by Leo Butler (Oran Mor / National Tour).

As Trainee Associate Director of Paines Plough, directing credits include HOUSE OF AGNES by Levi David Addai, THE DIRT UNDER THE CARPET by Rona Munro, CRAZY LOVE by Ché Walker, MY LITTLE HEART DROPPED IN COFFEE by Duncan Macmillan and BABIES by Katie Douglas.

Further directing credits include 2ND MAY 1997 by Jack Thorne (Bush Theatre), TERRE HAUTE by Edmund White (59East59 Theatres New York, West End, National Tour and Assembly Rooms, Edinburgh Festival Fringe), IS EVERYONE OK? and PUBLIC DISPLAYS OF AFFECTION by Joel Horwood and CAMARILLA by Van Badham (nabokov).

Paines Plough

"Revered touring company Paines Plough" **Time Out**

Paines Plough is the UK's national theatre of new plays.
We commission and produce the best playwrights and tour their
plays far and wide. Whether you're in Liverpool or Lyme Regis,
Scarborough or Southampton, a Paines Plough show is coming
to a theatre near you soon.

"The lifeblood of the UK's theatre ecosystem" **The Guardian**

Paines Plough was formed in 1974 over a pint of Paines bitter in
the Plough pub. Since then we've produced more than 150 new
productions by world renowned playwrights like Stephen Jeffreys, Abi
Morgan, Sarah Kane, Mark Ravenhill, Dennis Kelly and Mike Bartlett.
We've toured those plays to hundreds of places from Manchester to
Moscow to Maidenhead.

*"That noble company Paines Plough,
de facto national theatre of new writing"* **The Daily Telegraph**

We celebrated 40 years of Paines Plough with our biggest, boldest,
furthest-reaching programme of work ever. Programme 2014 saw 12
productions touring to 54 places around the UK, featuring the work
of 104 playwrights.

"I think some theatre just saved my life"
@kate_clement on Twitter

Paines Plough Limited is a company limited by guarantee and a registered charity.
Registered Company no: 1165130
Registered Charity no: 267523

Paines Plough, 4th Floor, 43 Aldwych, London WC2B 4DN
+ 44 (0) 20 7240 4533
office@painesplough.com
www.painesplough.com

Follow @PainesPlough on Twitter
Like Paines Plough at facebook.com/PainesPloughHQ
Donate to Paines Plough at justgiving.com/PainesPlough

Paines Plough are:

Supported using public funding by
ARTS COUNCIL
ENGLAND

LOTTERY FUNDED

"A beautifully designed masterpiece in engineering… a significant breakthrough in theatre technology."
The Stage

Roundabout is Paines Plough's beautiful new portable in-the-round theatre. It's a completely self-contained 168-seat auditorium that flat packs into a single lorry and can pop up anywhere from theatres to school halls, sports centres, warehouses, car parks and fields.

We built Roundabout to enable us to tour to places that don't have theatres. For the next decade Roundabout will travel the length and breadth of the UK bringing the nation's best playwrights and a thrilling theatrical experience to audiences everywhere.

Roundabout was designed by Lucy Osborne and Emma Chapman at Studio Three Sixty in collaboration with Charcoalblue and Howard Eaton.

WINNER of Theatre Building of the Year at The Stage Awards 2014

"The @painesplough Roundabout venue wins most beautiful interior venue by far @edfringe."
@ChaoticKirsty on Twitter

"Roundabout is a beautiful, magical space. Hidden tech make it Turkish-bath-tranquil but with circus-tent-cheek. Aces."
@evenicol on Twitter

PENTABUS
RURAL THEATRE COMPANY

We are the nation's rural theatre company.

Our mission is to develop and produce quality new theatre about the contemporary rural world. To tour the country with plays that have local impact and national resonance. To turn up in village halls, theatres and people's digital backyards, connecting audiences nationwide.

"The excellent touring company Pentabus" **The Guardian**

Since 1974 we've produced 150 new plays, supported 100 playwrights and reached over half a million audience members. We've won awards, pioneered live-streaming and developed a ground-breaking initiative to nurture young writers from rural backgrounds.

Our plans for the future will see us tour further than ever before, work with new and established playwrights, extend our young writers programme and continue to push at the boundaries of what theatre can be.

Pentabus is a registered charity (number 287909).
We rely on the generosity of our donors, small and large,
to help us to make brilliant new theatre.

You can find out more about us at www.pentabus.co.uk

Twitter @pentabustheatre

Facebook Pentabus Theatre

Supported using public funding by

ARTS COUNCIL
ENGLAND

LOTTERY FUNDED

Pentabus are:

Artistic Director	Elizabeth Freestone
Managing Director	Francesca Spickernell
Admin and Audience Development	Crayg Ward
Projects Producer	Jenny Pearce
Freelance Producer	Verity Overs-Morrell
Channel 4 Writer-in-Residence	Joe White
Associate Artist	Simon Longman
Bookkeeper	Lynda Lynne
Volunteer	Mike Price
Technical Stage Manager	Sam Eccles

Pentabus Theatre Company, Bromfield, Ludlow, Shropshire, SY8 2JU

Pentabus is also supported by The Millichope Foundation

EVERY BRILLIANT THING

Duncan Macmillan

with

Jonny Donahoe

OBERON BOOKS
LONDON

WWW.OBERONBOOKS.COM

First published in 2015 by Oberon Books Ltd
521 Caledonian Road, London N7 9RH
Tel: +44 (0) 20 7607 3637 / Fax: +44 (0) 20 7607 3629
e-mail: info@oberonbooks.com
www.oberonbooks.com

A catalogue record for this book is available from the British
Library.

PB ISBN: 978-1-78319-143-7
E ISBN: 978-1-78319-642-5

Cover design by Benedict Lombe

Printed, bound and converted
by CPI Group (UK) Ltd, Croydon, CR0 4YY.

Visit www.oberonbooks.com to read more about all our books
and to buy them. You will also find features, author interviews and
news of any author events, and you can sign up for e-newsletters
so that you're always first to hear about our new releases.

For Dad

Acknowledgements

George Perrin and Jonny Donahoe.

Anne McMeehan and Jim Roberts.

James Grieve, Elizabeth Freestone, Alicia White, Hanna Streeter, Francesca Moody, Benedict Lombe, Natalie Adams, Tara Wilkinson, Claire Simpson, Aysha Powell.

Jean Doumanian, Scott Morfee, Tom Wirtshafter, Patrick Daly, Preston Copley, Saul Nathan-Kazis, Kathryn Willingham, Kate Morrow, Victoria Gagliano, Amy Dalba, Richard Hodge, Charlene Speyerer, Matt Allamon, Josh Kohler.

Rosie Thomson, Ace Lawson, the Miniaturists, the Apathists, Lucy Prebble, Gugu Mbatha-Raw, Paul Burgess, Simon Daw, Kanatip LoukGolf Soonthornrak, Tom Dingle, Jamie Cullum, Sophie Dahl, Poppy Corbett, Ali Mason, Emma Campbell-Jones, Imogen Kinchin, Camilla Kinchin, Sian Reese-Williams, Stef O'Driscoll, Sean Linnen, Dominic Kennedy, Becki Willmore, Nikole Beckwith, Tom Richards, Robert Icke, Katie Mitchell, Josie Long, Daniel Kitson, Mark Thomas, Jessica Amato.

Mike Bartlett, Clare Lizzimore.

Paddy Gervers, Anna Knight.

Will Young. Rachel Taylor.

Michelle Beck. Effie Woods.

The play also owes a debt to those who have contributed to the list over the years.

Every Brilliant Thing is a collaboration between myself, George Perrin and Jonny Donahoe. It is an adaptation of my short story 'Sleeve Notes', originally written for the Miniaturists and performed by Rosie Thomson at Southwark Playhouse, Theatre503 and the Union Theatre and by myself at Trafalgar Studios, the Old Red Lion and Village Underground, by Gugu Mbatha-Raw at 93 Feet East and by various people at the Latitude Festival. George and I worked for over a decade to turn it into a full-length play. During this time it has been through several incarnations, including an installation created by Paul Burgess and Simon Daw for Scale Project. This particular incarnation was developed with Paines Plough and Pentabus with support from Anne McMeehan and Jim Roberts. The play wouldn't exist were it not for George's persistence, his enthusiasm for the story and his openness to work in an entirely new way.

It also owes a particular debt to Jonny Donahoe who, drawing on his experience as a stand-up comedian, found ways to tell the story and use the audience that George and I couldn't have conceived of. By its nature, the play is different every night and, as such, Jonny essentially co-authored the play while performing it.

This text was published after two years of devising, several trial performances around the UK, runs in Edinburgh and London and a four-month run at the Barrow Street Theatre in NYC. It has been filtered through Jonny's interactions with hundreds of audiences. I've provided footnotes throughout to explain certain aspects of the play in performance and to give examples of some of the things that have happened unexpectedly.

DM

Note

The NARRATOR can be played by a woman or a man of any age or ethnicity. In the first production, the NARRATOR was performed by a man, so appears as such in the text. The play should always be set in the country it's being performed in and references should be amended to reflect this.

The word NARRATOR is included for ease of reading. It is never heard by the audience and shouldn't be included in programmes or production materials.

There is no interval.

*****

The houselights are on full and will remain so throughout. There is no set. The AUDIENCE are seated in the most democratic way possible, ideally in the round. It is vital that everyone can see and hear each other. Music is playing, some upbeat jazz – Cab Calloway, Cannonball Adderley, Hank Mobley or Duke Ellington perhaps. The NARRATOR is in the auditorium as the AUDIENCE enters, talking to people and giving them scraps of paper. As he does so, he explains that when he says a number he wants the person with the corresponding entry to shout it out.[1]

Eventually, when everyone is seated, the music fades and the NARRATOR begins.

NARRATOR   The list began after her first attempt. A list of everything brilliant about the world. Everything worth living for.

1.   Ice cream.
2.   Water fights.
3.   Staying up past your bedtime and being allowed to watch TV.
4.   The colour yellow.
5.   Things with stripes.
6.   Rollercoasters.
7.   People falling over.

All things that, at seven, I thought were really good but not necessarily things Mum would agree with.

I started the list on the 9th of November, 1987.[2] I'd been picked up late from school

---

1   The AUDIENCE will be involved throughout and need to feel relaxed and safe. Greeting them also helps the NARRATOR cast the play. Jonny would be in the theatre for at least half an hour before the start of the show to speak to as many people as possible and work out who he was going to use in performance. The pieces of paper should look like authentic parts of the list – ones written during childhood could be written in crayon for instance, others should be written on napkins, beermats and the backs of envelopes (for example).

2   This date should be amended to correspond to the NARRATOR's age.

and taken to hospital, which is where my
Mum was.

,

Up until that day, my only experience of
death was that of my dog, Sherlock Bones.[3]

Sherlock Bones was older than me, and he
was a central part of my existence. He was
really sick and so the Vet came around to put
him down.

The NARRATOR speaks to someone from the AUDIENCE.

Would you mind, I'm going to get you
to be the Vet, it's just that you have an
immediate… *Veterinary* quality.

The NARRATOR gets the VET to stand.[4]

It's alright, I won't ask you to do very much.
Just stand here.

And would you mind if I borrowed your
coat?

The NARRATOR takes a coat from someone else.

Thank you.

Okay, so you're the Vet, and I'm me as a
seven-year-old boy, and this here…

*The NARRATOR holds the coat carefully in his arms, as
if it's a docile animal.*

…this is Sherlock Bones. I know you because
you're one of the parents from school. And
you say something reassuring, like:

---

3   Originally the dog's name was Ronnie Barker but we had to change that for the
    US. Other possible names included Charles Barkley and Edward Woofwoof.
4   The Vet can be a man or a woman.

>   *'You're doing the kind thing. It's not a moment too
>   soon.'*

VET   You're doing the kind thing. It's not a
                   moment too soon.[5]

NARRATOR   And I don't know what that means because
                   I'm seven. I've no real concept of finality. Or
                   mercy.

                   But you are clearly a very kind man, so I
                   trust you.

                   Now do you have a pencil or a pen on you?

*The VET has one or the NARRATOR asks him to get one
from someone in the AUDIENCE.[6]*

                   So that pencil is the needle.

                   And inside that needle is an anaesthetic
                   called pentobarbital. The dose is large
                   enough to make the dog unconscious and
                   then depress his brain, respiratory and
                   circulatory systems, and to put him to sleep
                   forever.

                   (To the owner of the coat.) It's completely blunt
                   so we won't draw on your nice coat okay?

                   When you're ready I want you to come over
                   here and inject Sherlock Bones in the thigh.

*The VET approaches the NARRATOR and attempts the
task.*

                   No, the thigh.

If the VET is smiling or laughing:

Now I'm going to stop you for a moment
there. There is one hard and fast rule while
euthanising a child's pet and that is you
really mustn't laugh as you do it. Totally
changes the tone of the situation.

So um, no…let's do this again. Go back to
the start and try to respect the solemnity of
the situation.

Maybe take a moment.

Okay. Let's try this again.

The VET completes the task.

Okay, now stroke his little head.

Could someone with a watch tell me when
thirty seconds has passed?

I held Sherlock Bones, who I'd known my
entire life. I held him as he died.

The NARRATOR looks at the coat, stroking it gently.

And I thought about the walk we'd had that
morning. And about the smell of him in my
room. His toys in the garden. The recently
opened packet of dry food. His bed under
the stairs. All the things that could now be
thrown away.

The NARRATOR looks at the coat for a little longer.

And he became lighter. Or heavier, I'm not
sure. But different.

*An AUDIENCE MEMBER tells the NARRATOR that thirty
seconds have passed.*

And that was my experience of death.

A loved one, becoming an object…

The NARRATOR hands the coat to the VET.

…and being taken away forever.

Thank you.

The VET returns to their seat.

It's the 9th of November, 1987. It's dark and it's late. All the other kids had gone home long ago.

Eventually, my Dad pulls up.

The NARRATOR speaks to someone in the AUDIENCE.

I'm going to ask you to be my Dad if that's okay. You don't have to do much, just sit here on this step.

The NARRATOR indicates where DAD should sit.[7]

Now, normally it's my Mum who picks me up and normally she's on time. Normally I travel in the back because I am seven and I make things sticky.

But this time it's Dad. And it's late. And he opens the door to the front passenger seat.

The NARRATOR indicates to DAD to open an imaginary passenger door.[8]

Dad looked at me. I looked at him.

---

7   If the DAD can be seen by everyone, and if the NARRATOR can sit next to him, there's no need for him to move.

8   In the US Jonny would correct DAD: 'Actually, it's a British car, so –' and they would mime opening the other door.

When something bad happens, your body feels it before your brain can know what's happening. It's a survival mechanism. The stress hormones cortisol and adrenalin flood your system. It feels like a trapdoor opening beneath you. Fight or flight or stand as still as you can.

I stood very still, looking at my Dad.

Eventually, I got into the car. Dad had the radio on. He'd been smoking with the window down.

The NARRATOR sits down next to the man.

Now, actually what's going to happen is that I'm going to be my Dad and you're going to be me as a seven year old. You don't have to do much, you just say 'why'. Okay?

The NARRATOR speaks as the DAD. He doesn't alter his voice.

DAD	Put on your seatbelt.
AUDIENCE	Why?
DAD	Because cars can be dangerous.
AUDIENCE	Why?
DAD	Because other drivers don't always pay attention.
AUDIENCE	Why?
DAD	Well, because there's lots to think about when you're a grown up. There are bills to pay and work to do and relationships to sustain and there's never enough time to do it all.
AUDIENCE	Why?

DAD	Because there are only twenty-four hours in a day.
AUDIENCE	Why?
DAD	Well, because that's how long it takes for the Earth to rotate.
AUDIENCE	Why?
DAD	Because…I don't know.
AUDIENCE	Why?
DAD	Because I don't know everything.
AUDIENCE	Why?
DAD	Because that's impossible.
AUDIENCE	Why?
DAD	Because there's only so much anyone can know.
AUDIENCE	Why?
DAD	Because if you were able to know everything then life would be unlivable.
AUDIENCE	Why?
DAD	Because then there would be no mystery, no curiosity, no creativity, no conversation, no discovery. Nothing would be new and we'd have no need to use our imaginations and our imaginations are what make life bearable.
AUDIENCE	Why?
DAD	Because in order to live in the present we have to be able to imagine a future that will be better than the past.

AUDIENCE	Why?
DAD	Because that's what hope is and without hope we couldn't go on.
AUDIENCE	Why?
DAD	Because…can you just put your seatbelt on?
AUDIENCE	Why?
DAD	Because we're going to the hospital.
AUDIENCE	Why?
DAD	Because that's where your mother is.
AUDIENCE	Why?
DAD	Because she hurt herself.
AUDIENCE	Why?
DAD	Because she's sad.
AUDIENCE	Why?
DAD	I don't know.
AUDIENCE	Why?
DAD	I just don't.
AUDIENCE	Why?
DAD	Put on your seatbelt.
AUDIENCE	Why?
DAD	Because your mother is in hospital.
AUDIENCE	Why?
DAD	Because she can't see anything worth living for.

AUDIENCE   Why?

                ,

NARRATOR   At least, that's how I like to remember it. But
                we actually just sat in silence. The only thing
                he said to me was:

                The NARRATOR feeds the 'DAD' the following line:

DAD   Your Mother's done something stupid.

NARRATOR   I didn't know what that meant.

                ,

                *The NARRATOR thanks the DAD and, if relocated,
                indicates for him to return to his seat.*

                At the hospital, Mum saw me and said 'not
                him'. So I sat in the corridor next to an old
                couple…

                *The NARRATOR sits next to an OLD COUPLE in the
                audience.*

                …who bought me a carton of juice and some
                chocolate from the machine.

                *He acquires a drink and some chocolate from the OLD
                COUPLE.[9]*

                I don't know exactly when I had the idea for
                the list but it was here, with the old people,
                that I started to write it down.

                The NARRATOR eats the chocolate and calls out numbers.

---

9   In performance 'chocolate and juice from a machine' changed depending on
    what could be acquired from the AUDIENCE – 'a cup of tea and a sandwich' for
    instance, or 'some water and an apple.' These then have to be included as items
    8 and 9. Jonny would often take someone's wine and react as a child would,
    saying 'spicy' and handing it back. In New York, we shortened it to just 'choco-
    late' and Jonny would hand one of the couple a bar of chocolate and then hold
    out his hand to get it back.

1.   Ice cream.
2.   Water fights.
3.   Staying up past your bedtime and being allowed to watch TV.
4.   The colour yellow.
5.   Things with stripes.
6.   Rollercoasters.
7.   People falling over.

The NARRATOR does the following entries himself.

8.   Juice.
9.   Chocolate.
10. Kind old people who aren't weird and don't smell unusual.

I don't like it.

The NARRATOR hands the drink and chocolate back to the OLD COUPLE.

Dad was in with Mum for ages. When he finally came out I followed him down the corridor, I followed him out of the hospital, I followed him to the car park, I followed him in to the car, I followed him up the driveway, I followed him in through the front door, I followed him down the hallway, I followed him up the stairs until we reached his study, where he went inside and closed the door before I could follow him any further.

I waited to see what music he put on.

I knew the rules. If it was this woman singing I could go into the room.

'Gloomy Sunday' by Billie Holiday plays, beginning with her vocal.

If it was the sort of music you could sing and dance to, it was okay to go in but I ran the risk of being hugged and spun around in his chair.

Some upbeat vocal jazz plays – Cab Calloway perhaps.

If no one was singing it meant Dad was working so I should be quiet.

Some melodic instrumental jazz plays, John Coltrane or Bill Evans perhaps.

And it if sounded like all the instruments were just falling down the stairs, it meant I should leave him alone.

'Free Jazz' by Ornette Coleman plays – loud and chaotic. After a moment it fades to silence.

,

So standing outside his door, I waited to see what he put on.

,

'Free Jazz' by Ornette Coleman plays. After a moment it fades.

I went downstairs and made myself some dinner. A ham and mayo sandwich. Just without the ham. I sat down in front of the TV and continued with the list.

It occurred to me the list should be presented in no particular order. There was no way of saying that, for example, Danger Mouse was objectively better than Spaghetti Bolognese.

23. Danger Mouse.
24. Spaghetti Bolognese.
25. Wearing a cape.
26. Peeing in the sea and nobody knows.

I stayed up late writing and fell asleep in the living room. Dad must have carried me upstairs.

Mum didn't come home for a week or so.

While she was away I had to speak to the school counsellor, which was actually just Mrs Patterson from upper school. She was a wonderful woman, the sort of woman you looked at and immediately trusted.

The NARRATOR looks at a woman in the AUDIENCE.

I'm going to ask you to be Mrs Patterson if that's okay. Now, what she'd do is, and it seems a little weird now but remember this was the Eighties and she got results, what she'd do is she'd take off her shoe...

The NARRATOR waits for MRS PATTERSON to take off her shoe. [10]

Then she'd take off her sock.

The NARRATOR waits for her to take off her sock. [11]

Then she'd put it on her hand and talk to you through her little sock-dog which she called – what did you call the sock-dog?

The AUDIENCE member says a name, for instance 'Mostyn'.

---

10 So far, nobody has refused to do this. In performance it sometimes took quite a while however. Jonny would acknowledge this, saying things like 'she liked to create a real sense of dramatic tension. She was a double-knotter, that's one of the things we always liked about her, very thorough.'

11 At one performance, MRS PATTERSON explained that she had a bad toe. Jonny added 'I remember her telling me how worried she was about her toe. It was a skydiving accident wasn't it?' MRS PATTERSON replied 'Yes that's right.' Jonny then included her in the list '165, Mrs Patterson and her extreme sports hobbies.'

	Yes! That's it, I remember now. What Mostyn would do is he'd ask questions like 'how are you feeling today?'
SOCK	How are you feeling today?
NARRATOR	I'm very well thank you Mostyn, how are you?
SOCK	I'm fine, thank you.
NARRATOR	You're brilliant. What kind of dog are you?
SOCK	I'm a... *(She specifies a breed or colour.)*
NARRATOR	Wow, that's amazing. When I was little we had a dog called Sherlock Bones, and he was a cross between a Border Collie and a Doberman, because a Border Collie and a Doberman lived next door to each other in our street and there was a very low hedge.

You're brilliant, by the way. I really like you. I'm going to put you onto my list. 164. Mostyn the sock dog. Have I told you about my list? |
| SOCK | No, tell me about it.[12] |
| NARRATOR | I'm making a list of a thousand Brilliant Things. I'm not certain but I think I might be a genius. |

If MRS PATTERSON wishes to ask more questions that's fine, if not the NARRATOR moves on to:

It's been very nice talking to you, but can I go now?

---

12 Occasionally, the sock dog would say that, yes, he had mentioned the list to which Jonny would reply something like 'well, I'd still like to recap'.

SOCK   Yes.[13]

NARRATOR   Mum did eventually come home from the
                        hospital, and by that time the list was eight
                        pages long and had three hundred and
                        fourteen things on it. I left it on her pillow
                        with the title:

                        'Every Brilliant Thing.'

                        She never mentioned it to me, but I knew
                        she'd read it because she'd corrected my
                        spelling.

                        ,

                        I kept speaking with Mrs Patterson and
                        Mostyn once a week, then once a fortnight,
                        then once a month and then one day I left
                        the school and I never saw them again.

                        I don't want to make it sound like my
                        Mother was a monster or that my childhood
                        was miserable because it wasn't.

                        We had a piano in our kitchen. It wasn't a
                        big kitchen but it was the warmest room in
                        the house and we'd gather around it and
                        sing soul songs. There's a Ray Charles song,
                        'Drown In My Own Tears' that she sang a
                        lot. There's a moment halfway through that
                        sends shivers down my spine.

                        This moment of the song plays – the drums building
                        and Ray Charles singing 'why can't YOU...' The song
                        continues, quieter.

                        The way he sings the word 'you' gets me
                        every time. It's like it's coming out of

13 If the SOCK/MRS PATTERSON insist that the NARRATOR stay and talk, the NAR-
    RATOR can beg childishly until they are released.

someone else. We all used to howl it like
wolves.

313.   Having a piano in the kitchen.
314.   The way Ray Charles sings the word
         'You'.

*The music swells and continues to play for a few moments
longer. The* NARRATOR *listens. It fades.*

I forgot about the list until her second
attempt, just over ten years later.

Dad showed up halfway through Chemistry.
The same trapdoor feeling. Fight or flight.
The same wordless drive to the hospital.

As a teenager I dealt with it less well. I wore
my heart on my sleeve.

The night she came home, she sat at the
kitchen table and said that if it wasn't for the
ham and pineapple pizza lining her stomach
from the night before she'd be dead. And I
said:

*'You took three weeks' worth of anti-depressants, a
packet of Aspirin and half a tub of antihistamines.
You're probably healthier than I am. If you're
going to kill yourself go jump off a bridge.'*

Rather than storm off I sat there and started
to shovel food into my mouth. I'd spent
ages on this meal and I was furious that she
was sitting there, wishing she was dead and
letting it go cold.

There was a moment of absolute, deafening
silence. And then she started to laugh. It
was such a genuine laugh that after a while I
found myself joining in. Eventually, Dad got

up and left the table, going into his study to listen to records.

I couldn't sleep that night. I started to clear out my room, packing up the things I wanted to keep and throwing away the things I didn't.

I started shaking. Have you ever had that? Where you notice that your hands are shaking and your breathing is deeper and you're surrounded by bin bags full of your things and you realise that, you know, *I'm really upset.* I must be really upset.

,

And then, inside a box under my bed, underneath some sticker albums, sea shells and action figures, I found the list. I sat on the floor and I read it through.

1.   Ice cream.

The younger me had dealt with this so much better. He wasn't self-righteous. The younger me was hopeful. Naïve, of course. But, hopeful.

So once I got to the end of the list I picked up a pen and continued where that little boy had left off.

315.   The smell of old books.
316.   Andre Agassi.
317.   The even numbered Star Trek films.
318.   Burning things.
319.   Laughing so hard you shoot milk out of your nose.
320.   Making up after an argument.

The next morning I sat at the end of Mum's
bed and I read the list to her, and she got up
and left the room. I followed her and read
louder.

516. Winning something.
517. Knowing someone well enough to get
them to check your teeth for broccoli.

Over the next few days and weeks I would
leave messages on the answer phone. I
would turn off the radio or stand in front of
the TV. I spent a lot of time talking to her
back.

518. When idioms coincide with real-
life occurrences, for instance:
waking up, realising something and
simultaneously smelling coffee.
521. The word 'plinth'.

I began leaving Post-It notes around the
house, stuck to various things. On her mirror
was:

575. Piglets.

On the kettle:

654. Marlon Brando.

And on her bed:

11. Bed.

Every morning I would open my door and I
would see a small stack of yellow squares of
paper. I became more inventive, writing on
the inside of cereal packets or shoes, carving
words into fruit or rearranging the fridge
magnets.

201.   Hammocks.

…inside the lid of some mustard.[14]

324.   Nina Simone's voice.

…stencilled onto a baguette.

It was my aim to reach a *thousand*. I wasn't
allowed to cheat, which meant:

a.   No repetition.
b.   Things had to be genuinely wonderful
     and life-affirming.
c.   Not too many material items.

For a few months the list became my sole
focus.

761.   Deciding you're not too old to climb
       trees.
823.   Skinny dipping.

Then, the week before I left for university:

992.   Knowing to jangle keys at the wildlife
       park if you want the otters to come
       out.
993.   Having dessert as a main course.
994.   Hairdressers who listen to what you
       want.
995.   Bubble wrap.
996.   Really good oranges.

I started to be bothered by the thought that
my Mum no longer loved my Dad. I put the
thought out of my mind and returned to the
list.

997.   Cycling downhill.

---

14   In George's production, this entry was written on an actual mustard lid.

998.   Aromatic duck pancakes with hoisin
        sauce.

It's common for the children of suicides to
blame themselves. It's natural.

999.   Sunlight.

However much you know that you're not to
blame, you can't help feeling like you failed
them. It's not fair to feel this way. But it's
natural.

,

In the first week of university, I posted the
list to my Mum, anonymously.[15] When I
returned that Christmas I found it on my
desk, neatly folded back in its envelope. I
still don't know whether or not she had read
it. It certainly hadn't seemed to change her
outlook.

I put the list between the pages of a favourite
book and I forgot about it.

That Christmas was quiet. Difficult.

In the New Year, Dad drove me back to
university. He gave me a box of his records.
I wanted to ask him why but I knew better
than that. We didn't speak. We just listened
to the radio.

*The NARRATOR sits down next to the person he cast as
his DAD.*

---

15 Jonny would often tell the AUDIENCE how he uses this joke as a barometer for
    how the show was going, sometimes telling them: 'they don't laugh at that in
    the matinees.'

Music plays – Ella Fitzgerald's 'My Melancholy Baby.' They listen for a moment, then it fades slowly as the NARRATOR speaks.

I was quite shy at university. I didn't socialise. I'd mostly just listen to records in my room. I would even avoid lectures and seminars. But there was one lecture series that I never missed.

It was lead by someone whose books I had read and loved and had inspired me to choose the course in the first place.

Would you mind being my lecturer? It's just because you really look like her.[16]

The NARRATOR selects someone from the audience to be the LECTURER, leads them to the centre of the room and gives them a copy of The Sorrows of Young Werther.

This particular lecture series was on the Victorian Novella and built up to this one book, *The Sorrows of Young Werther* by Johann Wolfgang von Goethe.

What she would do is, at the start of the lecture, she would hold the book aloft...

The LECTURER holds up the book.

And then she would leave a long dramatic pause...

...and when she felt she had everybody's undivided attention...

16 The LECTURER can be a man or a woman. Jonny would often describe the lecturer first, explaining that they always wore red-rimmed glasses for instance, before asking someone who is dressed exactly how he's just described to take part, saying 'I don't know why, but you really remind me of her...'

'

    …she would give a very accurate and
    detailed précis of the novel.

The NARRATOR sits in the audience and waits.

'

*Eventually, the LECTURER realises they can simply read
the plot summary on the back of the book. The summary
will be different depending on the copy, but will basically
say something like:*

LECTURER   Visiting an idyllic German village, Werther,
    a sensitive young man, meets and falls in
    love with sweet-natured Lotte. Although
    he realises that she is to marry Albert,
    he is unable to subdue his passion and
    his infatuation torments him to the point
    of despair. The first great 'confessional'
    novel, *The Sorrows of Young Werther* draws
    both on Goethe's own unrequited love for
    Charlotte Buff and on the death of his friend
    Karl Wilhelm Jerusalem. The book was
    an immediate success, and a cult rapidly
    grew up around it, resulting in numerous
    imitations as well as violent criticism and
    suppression on the grounds of its apparent
    support of suicide.

The NARRATOR puts his hand up.

NARRATOR   Excuse me, I have a question.

LECTURER   Yes?

NARRATOR   Are you saying that a book, that this book,
    caused people to take their own lives?

LECTURER   Yes.

NARRATOR	And you want *us* to read that book?
LECTURER	Yes.

The NARRATOR thanks the LECTURER and indicates for them to return to their seat.

,

NARRATOR	I left the lecture and went to the library.

I read up on social contagions; obesity, divorce, suicide. We're all subconsciously affected by the behaviour of our peers.

In the month after Marilyn Monroe's death by overdose, the number of suicides in the US increased by twelve percent. Every time suicide is front-page news, every time a celebrity or a character on prime-time television takes their own life there is a spike in the number of suicides.

Suicide is contagious. It's called the 'Werther Effect', named after Goethe's protagonist.

Discovering this fact really scared me. Then it made me angry. I thought about the way suicide was presented in films and on TV, how it was reported in the news.

I found that the Samaritans had published a set of guidelines for how the media can report suicide intelligently. It's astonishing how rarely these guidelines are followed. They're really simple:

The NARRATOR refers to a piece of paper.

Don't provide technical details. Never suggest that a method is quick, easy, painless or certain to result in death.

28

Avoid dramatic headlines, terms like 'suicide epidemic' or 'hot spot'.

Avoid sensationalist pictures of video. Avoid excessive detail.

Avoid using the word 'commit'. Don't describe deaths by suicide as 'successful'.

Don't publish suicide notes.

Don't publish on the front page.

Don't ignore the complex realities of suicide and its impacts on those left behind.

Include references to support groups, such as the Samaritans.

Don't speculate on the reason. That's crucial.

The NARRATOR puts away the paper.

Don't supply simplistic reasons such as 'he'd lost his job' or 'she'd recently become bankrupt'.

I read the book. *The Sorrows of Young Werther.* It was shit. Well, I didn't connect with it. I'd never been very interested in romance. Or at least, I hadn't been. Until I locked eyes with the only other person who was always in the library.

'At Last' by Etta James begins to play and the NARRATOR locks eyes with an AUDIENCE MEMBER. This is now SAM.[17] The NARRATOR waves, blushingly. The vocal starts and the song continues as the NARRATOR speaks.

---

17   SAM can be male or female. For the purpose of this draft, it's a woman.

For weeks we would sit opposite each other without speaking. Occasionally we'd make eye-contact and then immediately look away as if blinded by the sun.

For the first time in my life I understood the lyrics of pop songs.

And then finally, after weeks, I summoned-up the courage to say hello.

Slowly, bashfully, the NARRATOR walks towards SAM. On his way he asks the person who read out 517 to check his teeth for broccoli, then gives The Sorrows of Young Werther *to someone else.*

Can you just...deal with this?

As he is about to reach SAM, he suddenly turns to the person next to her.

Can I move you?

The NARRATOR gets the person next to SAM (usually their partner) to vacate their seat and move to the other side of the room. This is done very apologetically. Once relocated, the NARRATOR returns to SAM.

Is anyone sitting here?

SAM   Not anymore.

NARRATOR   Oh good.

The NARRATOR sits down in the empty seat.

Hello.

SAM   Hello.

NARRATOR   What's your name?

The AUDIENCE MEMBER says their name.

No, in real life her name was Sam.

What's your name?

SAM   Sam.

NARRATOR   Hi Sam. Nice to meet you. What are you reading?

The NARRATOR addresses the AUDIENCE.

Oh, I forgot, does anyone have a book? We're in the library so I need a couple of books.

The NARRATOR indicates The Sorrows of Young Werther.

Not that one.

The NARRATOR gets a couple of books from the AUDIENCE and throws one into SAM's lap.

What are you reading?

SAM reads the title of the book.[18]

What's it about?

SAM reads the back of the book.

Sounds really good.

---

18   Books that have been contributed by the AUDIENCE have included *God's Gift to Women*, *The Catcher in the Rye*, *Fifty shades of Grey* and *The Denial of Death* among many others.

The NARRATOR tells SAM what he's reading and tries to explain how great it is:[19]

It's really good. In fact, why don't I lend it to you? And I could read *(says title of SAM's book)* and we could meet up and talk about them, perhaps get a coffee sometime or a cup of tea or an or an or an orange juice, maybe, perhaps, if you'd like to, if you think that would be…[20]

SAM agrees.

I had a date! We began to meet up in the library. We'd swap books and discuss them over coffee. I read things I would never have encountered otherwise. I probably learned more from the books Sam gave me than from any of my course texts.

After several months of reading and meeting and trying not to look at each other, Sam returned a book to me, one of my favourite childhood books, and said:

---

19 Occasionally Jonny would be given the perfect book to start a flirtatious conversation – *Jane Eyre* for instance – and give the book's owner a big thumbs up. Most often though, he'd have a real struggle to make the book he's been given sound exciting. In one performance in New York he was given an enormous hardback history of Manhattan's sewage system. 'It's really…great' he enthused: 'You'd be surprised just how much there is to say about the history of Manhattan's sewage system. If you're going to read one book about the history of Manhattan's sewage system, it really should be this one.' He asked SAM if she had read the book and when she said she hadn't he replied 'No, of course not. No one has.' At one performance in Edinburgh Jonny was given *Nana* by Émile Zola, in French. This prompted him to turn to the person who'd contributed it and say 'aren't you clever?' and then add 'it's funny, for a minute I forgot I could speak French.' He then began to discuss the book with its owner in French, a language he happens to speak fluently. The conversation was cut short by the sign interpreter who was having a tough enough time as it was. During a press night performance he was given a copy of *Macbeth*, giving him a dilemma of whether or not to say the title out loud, given the circumstances. In London he was given a copy of my play *Lungs* which was playing in the same theatre. Aware that I was sitting directly behind him he explained that he thought it was okay if you're into babies and the environment but that he preferred the more recent stuff.

20 Jonny would just keep going here until SAM agreed.

The NARRATOR says the lines and encourages SAM to repeat them back to him.

NARRATOR   <u>Really</u> interesting read.

SAM   <u>Really</u> interesting read.

NARRATOR   There's something <u>really interesting</u> in this book…

SAM   There's something <u>really interesting</u> in this book…

NARRATOR   That I want <u>you</u> to read.

SAM   That I want <u>you</u> to read.

NARRATOR   Now, this confused me because I'd already read the book. *I'd* lent it to *her.* Because I'm an idiot, I didn't work out that it was code until weeks later, when I opened the book and the list dropped out.

             I was mortified. I'd never told anyone about my Mum. Ever. As a kid there were times when…I'd have nothing in my lunchbox or I wouldn't have socks on or something and I…I didn't want people to think that because my Mother was…I don't know. And out of context this was just a stupid, childish list. The idea that a list of nice things could combat hardwired depression was embarrassingly naïve.

             I got so upset I went to rip it in half…and then I noticed someone else's handwriting.

The NARRATOR says each number. SAM reads all the entries.

     1000.   When someone lends you books.

33

1001. When someone actually reads the books you give them.
1002. When you learn something about someone that surprises you but which makes complete sense.
1003. Realising that for the first time in your life someone is occupying your every waking thought, making it hard to eat or sleep or concentrate, and that they feel familiar to you even though they're brand new.
1004. Finding an opportunity to say this in a way which doesn't involve being in the same room at the same time, as we're both shy and terrified of rejection and if I don't say something now, it'll never happen.
1005. Writing about yourself in the Third Person.

I have some advice for anyone who has been contemplating suicide. It's really simple advice. It's this:

Don't do it.

Things get better.

They might not always get brilliant.

The NARRATOR indicates SAM.

But they get better.

,

What I'm about to say might be really hard for some of you to understand, particularly the younger members of the audience. Back then there was no way to communicate with anyone after midnight. No texting or instant messaging, no email or Facebook. This world was called '1998.'

I couldn't do anything but stare at what Sam had written. For about three hours.

Eventually, I just continued the list from where Sam had left off.

1006.   Surprises.
1007.   The fact that sometimes there is a perfect song to match how you're feeling.

Music begins: 'Move On Up' by Curtis Mayfield. The NARRATOR moves quickly around the room.[21]

1008.   Dancing in private.
1009.   Dancing in public, fearlessly.
1010.   Reading something which articulates exactly how you feel but lacked the words to express yourself.

I wrote late into the night.

1427.   Not worrying about how much money you're spending on holiday because all international currency looks like Monopoly money.

I wanted to get to 2000 and I kept writing as the sun came up.

1654.   Christopher Walken's voice.
1655.   Christopher Walken's hair.

So much to include that my hand cramped up.

---

21   In George's production, Jonny would use a microphone during this section, and get the AUDIENCE MEMBERS to speak into it too. This was partly so we could have the music loud but also to introduce a microphone that will be used later.

1857. Planning a declaration of love.

My morning alarm went but I'd not slept. I passed:

2000. Coffee.

With:

2001. Films that are better than the books they're adapted from.

And I kept going.

The NARRATOR does the following entries himself, at speed:

2002. Seeing someone make it onto the train just as the doors are closing, making eye-contact and sharing in this little victory.
2003. This song. Especially the drums on this track. The single ends at around four minutes but the album version continues for another five minutes and has the most insane drums. In fact...
2004. Any song with an extended drum break involving a full kit, bongos and cowbell, have you heard 'I'm a Man' by Chicago?
2005. 'I'm a Man' by Chicago.
2006. Vinyl records. I'm not being pretentious, the sound quality is better, it isn't compressed and it's tactile, you get to feel the weight of it in your hands. You can't skip like with CDs or MP3s, you listen through to the entire album. Dad's room had records on every surface and I loved the gatefold sleeves, the artwork, I love reading through the

acknowledgements and the sleeve notes, the story of the making of the object.

The next morning I took the list and I ran to the library and Sam and I kissed for the very first time.

From that moment on we spent every second together. I wrote new list entries every day as a gift for Sam.

The NARRATOR continues with the list entries himself:

2389. Badgers.

The NARRATOR puts his hand on someone's shoulder.

2390. People who can't sing but either don't know or don't care.

Pages and pages of it.

4997. Gifts that you actually want and didn't ask for.
4998. Falling asleep as soon as you get on a plane, waking up when you land and feeling like a time-traveller.

Everywhere I looked, everything I thought about...

9993. Dreams of flying.
9994. Friendly cats.
9995. Falling in love.
9996. Sex.
9997. Being cooked for.
9998. Watching someone watching your favourite film.
9999. Staying up all night talking.
10000. Waking up late with someone you love.

The drum-break kicks in.

Now, this is the drum break I was telling you about. I know what you're thinking: it just sounds like a bunch of drums but wait for it, you're about to hear…

The NARRATOR waits for it.

…bongos! You are not getting into this in the way I anticipated. Alright, fine, listen, I'm going to try to be a little bit more…American about this. Let's try…everyone put your right hand in the air.

Everyone raises their right hand.

I'm going to HIGH-FIVE THE ENTIRE ROOM!

He high-fives as many people as he can.

Eventually, the NARRATOR signals to the STAGE MANAGER to stop the record.

No that was a big mistake. It's actually much harder than I anticipated.

The NARRATOR is out of breath.

My Mum…

She would do this. Get carried away. Ups and downs.

,

As a little boy, it was never shyness, or thoughtfulness. Happiness scared me because it was usually followed by…

you know.

The NARRATOR looks at SAM.

This was all very new. Feeling like this.

,

Studies have shown that children with
depressed mothers have a heightened
reactivity to stress. Mothers who are
withdrawn leave children to fend for
themselves and it actually changes the
chemistry of the brain, the fight or flight
impulse.

But the real risk as I perceived it…

,

The real risk, that I'd felt my whole life, was
that I would one day feel as low as my Mum
had and take the same action.

Because alongside the anger and
incomprehension is an absolute crystal clear
understanding of why someone would no
longer want to continue living.

,

I took Sam back home to meet my parents.
They were amazing. They were wonderful.
They were fantastic. It was awful. It made it
seem like I'd exaggerated everything from
my childhood. My Dad made lasagne and
played Cab Calloway records. My Mum
laughed a lot and told a story about breaking
a guy's nose on a train in Egypt. We drank
a few bottles of wine and sang songs at the
kitchen piano.

*The NARRATOR produces an electric keyboard and stands
with it in the centre of the room. It doesn't have a stand,*

so for a moment he tries to work out how to play it. Then he recruits two people from the AUDIENCE to hold either end of it while he plays. He thinks about the logistics of the room and speaks to the people holding the keyboard.

Um, because we're in the round, we're just going to do a very slow revolve.

Clockwise, obviously.

The NARRATOR speaks to the room.

Mum would always sing first. She sang Ray Charles…

(Sings.) I'm so blue here without you
it keeps raining more and more. Why can't YOU…

Dad wouldn't normally sing. But he did this night. It was amazing. I'd never seen anything like it. He sang:

(Sings.) That's Life. That's what people say.
Riding High in April, shot down in May.

oh…and:

(Sings.) And now the end is near,
and so I face the final curtain.

Which, for me, was a little too on the nose.

And then, quite spectacularly:

(Sings.) Wake me up before you go-go,
don't leave me hangin' on like a yo-yo.

Which, because he'd clearly never heard it before, actually sounded like:

(Sings, to the tune of 'Fly Me To The Moon')
Wake me up before you go-go,
don't leave me hangin' on like a yo-yo.

Sam sang the last song that night. 'Some Things Last A Long Time' by Daniel Johnston. I'd not heard it before.

The NARRATOR sings a few lines of the song, ending:

(Sings.) The things we did, I can't forget.
Some things last a long time. Some things last a long time.

,

The NARRATOR takes away the piano and his assistants return to their seats.[22]

With Sam's encouragement, the list grew.

123321.   Palindromes.

People asked if they could read it, add to it, photocopy it. The document got scrawled all over with different handwriting in different colours, exclamation marks, underlining, asterisks, footnotes and amendments, drawings and even the odd diagram.

Anything generic or universal (clean sheets, new socks, freshly cut grass, the smell of bacon) had already been included and entries had become more specific:

253263.   The feeling of calm which follows the realisation that, although you may be in a regrettable situation, there's nothing you can do about it.

525924.   Track 7 on every great record.

777777.   The prospect of dressing up as a Mexican wrestler.

Not the *action* of dressing up as a Mexican Wrestler, but the *prospect* of it.

---

22   This should be done in a way to ensure that the audience don't applaud at this point.

Sam and I got married. A year after
university. Sam proposed. Got down on one
knee. The whole thing.

It was beautiful, it was…in fact, no, let's just
do it.

We were walking in a park near my parents'
house. It was raining. I was saying that this is
where I used to walk Sherlock Bones when
I was a child. I kept walking and I thought
she'd stopped to tie a shoelace because when
I turned around she was on one knee.

*The NARRATOR turns around to look at SAM, who is
down on one knee.*[23]

She took my hands and said…

SAM   Will you marry me?

NARRATOR   And I said yes.

Let's kiss later.

SAM returns to her seat.

We picked a date. Hired a hall. Caterers. Band.

Everyone was there. Even our old Vet. We
didn't invite him, but he came.[24]

Dad did a speech. It was the most wonderful,
beautiful speech I'd heard in my entire life.

And you know Dad, he hated public
speaking. I said to him, Dad, you really don't
have to say anything but he said…

---

23 In one performance in Edinburgh, the wonderful stand-up Josie Long was
    chosen to play SAM. At this point, she took a receipt from her pocket, fashioned
    it into a ring and used it to propose to Jonny. Jonny wore the ring for the rest of
    the performance.
24 It could be the VET or the LECTURER who crashes the wedding, whichever seems
    more amusing for the particular performance.

The NARRATOR gets the microphone, takes the DAD by the hand and leads him into the middle of the room.

...no I really want to. I really want to take this opportunity to talk to everyone, so...

The NARRATOR speaks into the microphone.

...Ladies and Gentlemen, in a break from tradition, please welcome the Father of the Groom.

The NARRATOR gives the DAD the microphone, asks him to wait for a moment, then sits next to SAM and links arms.

Say what's in your heart Dad.

The 'DAD' improvises a short speech, after which the NARRATOR hugs the DAD and lets them return to their seat.[25]

I remember every word.

After the reception, when most of the guests had gone home,[26] Mum sat at the piano and played soul songs.

The snippet of Ray Charles plays – 'Why can't YOU...'

,

After the wedding Sam and I went on holiday to Whitstable in Kent.[27] We were so

---

25 This is probably the most unpredictable moment of the play. Sometimes it's very brief, sometimes the NARRATOR needs to cut it short. It can be very funny or very emotional, such as the occasion when the DAD (who turned-out to be a real-life Rabbi) ended his speech with the words 'Son, you used to always ask me 'why?' and I never had an answer for you. Well, today I know that you have found your answer.'

26 Depending on the DAD's speech, this sometimes became 'After the speeches, once we'd all recovered...'

27 In America this often got a laugh, prompting Jonny to say 'that's not supposed to be funny. It's just where we went.'

43

happy. The sun shone every day. We ate the most incredible seafood.

We moved to London. We got jobs. A car. A joint bank account. A cat who peed on everything then ran away. We called her Margaret Scratcher. We settled into a routine. We saw less and less of each other. We were tired. We argued. We argued about money. We argued about whether we wanted to live in the city or the countryside. We argued about whether or not we should start a family.

We had one argument in particular.

Sam suggested that I talk to someone. Professionally.

That made me so angry. I knew what depression was and I knew I was fine.

I had a study at home and I'd sit in there, listening to records and reading the sleeve notes.

The lives of other people have always fascinated me. I always read the liner notes in record sleeves. The trials and traumas behind the music. Tortured geniuses.

Weldon Irvine. Albert Ayler. Ronnie Singer. Donny Hathaway. Amazing musicians. All took their own lives.

I'm so grateful to be ordinary.

Sam told me I was becoming morose. That I was isolating myself. Wallowing.

She encouraged me to carry on with the list, but I found it hard to notice new things.

826978.

,

826978.

,

826978.

,

The list ended, just one hundred and seventy
three thousand and twenty two short of a
million. It was finished. So I boxed it all up
and threw it away.

,

I sat in my study while Sam packed her
things. I helped her carry boxes to her car. I
stood in our doorway and she looked at me
from the car.

That horrible feeling when something is
broken and can't ever be fixed. The trapdoor
swinging open. Fight or flight or stay as still
as you can.

I'd been feeling like that for a long time.

,

I watched her drive away.

,

She left me a note, written in an album
sleeve. She knew that when I wanted to think
of her I'd look for the Daniel Johnston song
she sang at my parent's house and, as always,
I'd sit and read through the record sleeve.

Sam's note said that she loved me and that when I was ready we should try again.

But I didn't find the note for seven years.

,

Perhaps Sam had been right. Perhaps I'd been difficult to live with. Difficult to love.

But I couldn't hear it from her. I needed to talk to someone else.

So, the night I found Sam's note, I did one of the oddest things I've ever done.

,

Mrs Patterson?

MRS PATTERSON Yes.

NARRATOR   I hope you don't mind me calling you so late, I know you've retired, I know that because I called the school and they gave me your number. I know this is really inappropriate but…I'm an ex-pupil of yours. I was the little boy with the list. Do you remember me?

MRS PATTERSON Yes.

,

NARRATOR   You do?

MRS PATTERSON Yes.

,

NARRATOR   You used to have a sock puppet, do you remember?

MRS PATTERSON Yes.

NARRATOR   A black dog. Which, now I come to think of
                  it is a little ironic. Mostyn, wasn't it?

MRS PATTERSON Yes.

NARRATOR   I was always able to talk to Mostyn. This
                  may sound strange, but, would it be possible
                  to talk to Mostyn now?

                  *MRS PATTERSON takes off her shoe and her sock once
                  again and puts the sock over her hand.*

SOCK   Hello.

NARRATOR   Hello Mostyn. How're you?

SOCK   I'm fine, how're you?

NARRATOR   Well, I'm talking to a sock dog on the phone,
                  so apparently not great.

                  ,

                  I'm sad.

                  I'm really sad Mostyn and I don't know how
                  to change that. And I wanted to speak to you
                  because when I was a little boy you knew me
                  better than anyone.

                  I wanted to ask you: was I always like this?
                  Do you remember what I was like?

SOCK   Yes.

NARRATOR   Was I happy?

                  *The NARRATOR leads the SOCK PUPPET through a brief
                  conversation until a conclusion is reached that allows
                  the NARRATOR to take the next step – either he's always
                  been sad or he was once happy.*

                  ,

Thank you. It means a lot to hear that from you.

I'm sorry I called so late. I won't call you again. Goodnight.

MRS PATTERSON Goodnight.

,

NARRATOR I did talk to someone.

A group. A support group.

,

Hello everyone.

The NARRATOR indicates for everyone to respond.

AUDIENCE Hello.

NARRATOR This is my first session. I've resisted doing this.

I'm –

you know,

,

British.

I now realise that it's important to talk about things. Particularly the things that are the hardest to talk about.

When I was younger I was much better at being happy.

At feeling joy.

Being a grown-up, being conscious of the problems in the world, about the complexities, the tragedies, the disappointments…I'm not sure I can ever fully allow myself to be joyful. I'm just not very good at it. It's helpful to know there are other people who feel the same.

I um –

I made a list. Everything that's brilliant about the world.

I began making it as a present for my Mum. It's kind of a long story.

The list is –

Actually, wait a second, I have it with me…

The NARRATOR exits the stage, then returns with a trolley on which sit several large, heavy, worn boxes.

You see, I threw it away but, unbeknownst to me, my partner at the time…

The NARRATOR looks at SAM.

…got it out of the trash and hid it in the garage under an old tablecloth and then left a note about it in the record sleeve of a Curtis Mayfield record…well, you don't need to know the details.

He opens one of the boxes. It is full of scraps of paper, the list, written on pages of colouring books, on receipts and beer mats, on the backs of envelopes etc. He takes a moment to just look at it. He carefully takes out a stack and looks through it. He reads entries at random and drops them, scattering them on the floor.

Peeling off a sheet of wallpaper in one intact piece.

He reads another.

Mork and Mindy.

He holds up a sleeve from a shirt and reads what's written on it:

My new sleeveless top.

He reads another.

Old people holding hands.

,

He smiles and looks around the room.

If you live a long life and get to the end of it without ever once having felt crushingly depressed, then you probably haven't been paying attention.

,

I wasn't around for the last time. I was in Australia with work and when I got the call I was on the beach. Dad wasn't around either. A neighbour complained about the exhaust fumes and eventually the police cut through the garage door. Hosepipe through the driver-side window.

That surprised me actually, because Mum hated driving.

She had poor circulation and would always complain about her ankles on long journeys. They say that it's a masculine way to choose to die. But I don't know what that means.

There was a pad and pencil on the passenger seat but she hadn't written anything.

I drove Dad to the funeral. We sat in silence. He smoked with the window down. I helped him with his tie.

After the service, meeting my Mum's friends and colleagues, I realised how much the list had changed the way I see the world.

31. Birdsong.
45. Hugging.
341. Alcohol.
577. Tea and biscuits.
1092. Conversation.

The list hadn't stopped her. Hadn't saved her. Of course it hadn't.

,

I got a text from Sam.

The NARRATOR gives SAM his phone to read.

SAM I heard about your Mum.

I'm so sorry.

Give me a call.

Anytime.

I'd love to hear your voice.

Love,

Sam x

Ps. I heard the other day that Beyonce is related to the composer Gustav Mahler. It occurred to me that this is a fact that should be on your list. Truly a brilliant thing.

,

I stayed with Dad for a few months after the funeral. We'd spend the days walking or reading or listening to records. He'd fall asleep in his armchair and I'd sit at his desk and type up the list, starting at the very beginning.

1.   Ice cream.

It was a lot of work. Several weeks of sleepless nights. Once I got to the end I kept going from where I'd left off.

826979.   The fact that Beyonce is Gustav Mahler's eighth cousin, four times removed.[28]

I completed the list.

,

I printed it out and left it in Dad's chair. I drove back to London.

He never mentioned it directly, but when we spoke a few weeks later, he said 'thank you.'

DAD   Thank you.

NARRATOR   And he said 'I love you'.

DAD   I love you.

NARRATOR   I told him that sentimentality didn't suit him.

999997.   The alphabet.

999998.   Inappropriate songs played at emotional moments.

999999.   Completing a task.

---

28 Jonny would take this entry out of his pocket and give it to the person he'd moved away from SAM, then allow them to return to their seat.

The NARRATOR says the final entry.

1000000. Listening to a record for the first time. Turning it over in your hands, placing it on the deck and putting the needle down, hearing the faint hiss and crackle of the sharp metal point on the wax before the music begins, then sitting and listening while reading through the sleeve notes.

,

'Into Each Life Some Rain Must Fall' by Ella Fitzgerald and the Ink Spots plays.

The NARRATOR shakes hands with or hugs the members of the AUDIENCE who played the principal characters – the VET, LECTURER, MRS PATTERSON, DAD and SAM, indicating for applause to be directed to them and inviting them to bow.

The NARRATOR then bows and leaves. The list remains scattered around the stage so that the AUDIENCE can look through the box and read the entries.

The music continues to play as they exit.

by the same author

The Most Humane Way to Kill a Lobster
9781840025590

Monster
9781840027594

Lungs
9781849431453

Don Juan Comes Back from the War
Ödön von Horváth, in a version by Duncan Macmillan
9781849432542

1984
George Orwell, in a new adaptation created by
Duncan Macmillan and Robert Icke
9781783190614

WWW.OBERONBOOKS.COM

Follow us on www.twitter.com/@oberonbooks
& www.facebook.com/OberonBooksLondon